S0-CAT-593

Shared
Expectations

Management Master Series

William F. Christopher
Editor in Chief

Set 3: Customer Focus

Karl Albrecht
Delivering Customer Value: It's Everyone's Job

Robert King
Designing Products and Services That Customers Want

Wayne A. Little
Shared Expectations: Sustaining Customer Relationships

Gerald A. Michaelson
Building Bridges to Customers

Eberhard E. Scheuing
Creating Customers for Life

Ron Zemke
Service Recovery: Fixing Broken Customers

Shared
Expectations

Sustaining Customer
Relationships

Wayne A. Little

PRODUCTIVITY PRESS
Portland, Oregon

Management Master Series
William F. Christopher, Editor in Chief
Copyright © 1995 by Productivity Press, Inc.

All rights reserved. No part of this book may be reproduced or utilized in any form or by any means, electronic or mechanical, including photo-copying, recording, or by any information storage and retrieval system, without permission in writing from the publisher. Additional copies of this book are available from the publisher. Address all inquiries to:

Productivity Press
P.O. Box 13390
Portland, OR 97213-0390
United States of America
Telephone: 503-235-0600
Telefax: 503-235-0909
E-mail: staff@ppress.com

Book design by William Stanton
Cover illustration by Paul Zwolak
Graphics and composition by Rohani Design, Edmonds, Washington
Printed and bound by Data Reproductions Corporation in the United
    States of America

Library of Congress Cataloging-in-Publication Data
Little, Wayne A.
    Shared expectations : sustaining customer relationships / Wayne
A. Little.
        p.   cm. -- (Management master series)
    Includes bibliographical references.
    ISBN 1-56327-149-4 (hardcover)
    ISBN 1-56327-096-X (paperback)
    1. Customer relations. 2. Industrial procurement. I. Title.
II. Series.
HF5415.5.L58 1995
658.8'12—dc20   95-12450
                                                                    CIP

00 99 98 97 96 95 10 9 8 7 6 5 4 3 2 1

—CONTENTS—

PUBLISHER'S MESSAGE

The *Management Master Series* was designed to discover and disseminate to you the world's best concepts, principles, and current practices in excellent management. We present this information in a concise and easy-to-use format to provide you with the tools and techniques you need to stay abreast of this rapidly accelerating world of ideas.

World class competitiveness requires managers today to be thoroughly informed about how and what other internationally successful managers are doing. What works? What doesn't? and Why?

Management is often considered a "neglected art." It is not possible to know how to manage before you are made a manager. But once you become a manager you are expected to know how to manage and to do it well, right from the start.

One result of this neglect in management training has been managers who rely on control rather than creativity. Certainly, managers in this century have shown a distinct neglect of workers as creative human beings. The idea that employees are an organization's most valuable asset is still very new. How managers can inspire and direct the creativity and intelligence of everyone involved in the work of an organization has only begun to emerge.

Perhaps if we consider management as a "science" the task of learning how to manage well will be easier. A scientist begins with an hypothesis and then runs experiments to observe whether the hypothesis is correct. Scientists depend on detailed notes about the experiment—the timing, the ingredients, the amounts—and carefully record all results as they test new hypotheses. Certain things come to be known by this method; for instance, that water always consists of one part oxygen and two parts hydrogen.

We as managers must learn from our experience and from the experience of others. The scientific approach provides a model for learning. Science begins with vision and desired outcomes, and achieves its purpose through observation, experiment, and analysis of precisely recorded results. And then what is newly discovered is shared so that each person's research will build on the work of others.

Our organizations, however, rarely provide the time for learning or experimentation. As a manager, you need information from those who have already experimented and learned and recorded their results. You need it in brief, clear, and detailed form so that you can apply it immediately.

It is our purpose to help you confront the difficult task of managing in these turbulent times. As the shape of leadership changes, the *Management Master Series* will continue to bring you the best learning available to support your own increasing artistry in the evolving science of management.

We at Productivity Press are grateful to William F. Christopher and our staff of editors who have searched out those masters with the knowledge, experience, and ability to write concisely and completely on excellence in management practice. We wish also to thank the individual volume authors; Diane Asay, project manager; Julie Zinkus, manuscript editor; Karen Jones, managing editor; Lisa Hoberg and Mary Junewick, editorial support; Bill Stanton, design and production management; Susan Swanson, production coordination; Rohani Design, graphics, page design, and composition.

Norman Bodek
Publisher

PREFACE

This book is written for those who believe that meeting customers' needs is the only way to stay in business. It is for those who have a passion for this belief! This material will help your business. Small or big. Simple or complex. Local or global. New or old. In a few pages, you will benefit from the thoughts in this book. You will share a passion for delighting customers. Getting even one good idea will be worth your effort.

The thoughts in this book represent a flexible approach. You will be disappointed if you are expecting a rigid set of rules. You will find guidelines, not an exact recipe. The reason? Customers expect flexibility. Customers expect customization. Customers want to be treated individually. One size will not fit all. You will be able to use the information in this book to customize the tools that fit your needs and match those of your customers.

As a bonus you will also get ideas about how to help your own suppliers to be better than they think they can be. You will help them to delight you. The methods described in this book result in ideas you can use to create product and service differentiation that will provide a greater level of customer satisfaction. A great way to do business!

You will discover tools that you can use internally for many situations. A good one is the alignment of goals and objectives. Another is to establish performance expectations. Even to solve personnel problems!

Today, the trend is to establish strategic relationships or partnerships. Major companies are reducing the number of suppliers and creating real and meaningful partnerships. Outsourcing critical operations and strategic functions is commonplace. Business is transforming itself. We are observing an uncommon amount of trust in suppliers and by suppliers.

Trust is absolutely the most essential ingredient of any relationship. And that trust is not built by words—it is built by actions. It is easier to earn that trust when there is a mutual understanding of what is expected. In an individual relationship, constant exposure to values, needs, and behaviors builds a knowledge of what is expected. The same is true in business. The problem is that a typical business is made up of many individuals each with their own sets of values, needs, and their own styles of behavior. Reaching a common understanding of expectations can take some time. And expectations may change with the coming and going of personnel. Many techniques can be used to gather the information and intelligence needed to determine expectations. But there is no better way than just simply asking. Relationships are a two-way street and both asking and telling are needed.

Most of us have informal ways of asking and telling. We may get around to both eventually, but too often we don't. This book describes a very useful asking and listening process called *Shared Expectations,* which AT&T developed from a customer's suggestion. You will be able to tailor this process to your customers and give it your own "spin." And you will be able to use the process again and again.

The Shared Expectations process saves you lots of time. Time you can use to build profitable sales volume by solving real and present problems. Time you can use to think creatively about how you can exceed expectations. Time to think how you can delight your customer. Time to think about how you can build lifetime relationships with customers.

The process will increase your profits. Your customer will see you as a valued partner. One who shares the same goals and objectives for their business. One who helps them to delight their customers by understanding and meeting their expectations. And they will reward you for your efforts.

You will have more fun. Your role as a supplier will feel more like that of a partner. You will have a win-win relationship and the good feelings that go with being a winner.

1

SHARED EXPECTATIONS: A NEW CONCEPT FOR BUILDING LASTING CUSTOMER RELATIONSHIPS

WHAT TO EXPECT

Expect to get some ideas! This is not about rocket science. It is about common sense. Don't expect a tutorial on quality. The emphasis is on delighting customers, building lasting relationships, and knowing how you did it—and doing it again and again. You will learn about a simple concept and technique that is useful for managing all types of relationships.

If you are currently focusing on quality, you will get new ideas. These ideas will help you leverage your knowledge about the quality process. If you are not, you will find new reasons to learn to use quality tools and processes.

THE OPPORTUNITY

Customers want to be heard. They want suppliers and partners to listen. They want to be asked. And they want vendors to understand what they really mean. The evidence is overwhelming. There is a huge opportunity for both buyers and sellers to improve relationships—by listening. This is confirmed by a recent survey by ODI, a leading quality consulting firm.[1]

- Two-thirds of executives surveyed said quality and customer satisfaction are the keys to their company's success.

- 92 percent said their companies have at least started to implement quality efforts.

- But! The same executives said two-thirds of their key suppliers' quality efforts generated no results or less than expected.

- 62 percent said suppliers should make more effort to communicate with customers and understand their needs and expectations.

- Only 8 percent of the executives said their key suppliers consistently involved them in setting quality improvement objectives.

- Fewer than one-third believe their suppliers really understand their company's business goals and quality objectives.

Communicating, understanding, and acting on what we learn offers tremendous opportunity for all of us, from the CEO to the sales force. The opportunity is to:

- differentiate ourselves from competitors
- build lasting relationships
- form beneficial relationships
- create successes for each party

Opportunities exist all along the buying continuum, from the analyst to the decision maker, including the person with the veto power. Chapter 4 explains this continuum in detail.

FOR OPENERS

Understanding the tools and the language of the quality process is the minimum price of admission to take advantage of the opportunity. Most people in marketing and similar functions believe hard-core quality training and TQM activities are only for manufacturing and technical processes. When you do find quality programs in other functions, the focus is usually internal. And this is necessary to the learning process. In selling, however, the real action is when you can leverage your knowledge externally.

USING QUALITY TOOLS AND PROCESSES WITH CUSTOMERS

The quality effort was not new at AT&T, but it was relatively new to those in marketing and selling. We started by training all associates in quality awareness. Our first efforts were slow with many starts and stops and many changes of direction. Changing attitudes and learning is hard work. It can be a long, slow journey.

Many of your customers have been exposed to the quality process. Some are well along the way. They recognize that the quality of their product or service depends on the input of suppliers. They have already engaged their suppliers in the quality process. Others may be just starting. The entire range offers you an opportunity. If you are well-versed in the use of quality improvement techniques, you can play at any level. If you are not, you can make faster progress by starting with the customers who have established quality processes. They can help you learn and you, in turn, can then help your other customers with the quality process.

PLAYING YOUR CARDS

Many creative salespeople have discovered that their customers are in various stages of embracing the quality movement. Some are considering it and investigating how to start. Others are well on their way. And some are already sophisticated in the use of quality principles.

Early success can come simply by asking to join customer quality improvement teams working on processes your products and services touch. We were able to join with many customers because we understood the language and the tools. We could and did contribute. Other successes came when customers joined our quality teams. That is when we really began to learn and practice quality techniques.

Some customers were looking for help in starting quality programs. We were able to respond. We shared experiences and lent a helping hand. At the same time we underscored our commitment to the continuous improvement of our products, services, and processes. These efforts paid dividends.

WHAT IS THE PAYOFF?

Quality efforts that fail to enhance your competitive advantage are not functional, even if they make you and your associates feel great. Reaching out to key customers by joining in their efforts or inviting them to be partners in shaping your quality improvement is what really pays off. You will find you can focus on strategically important goals—theirs and yours. You will see and respond directly to your customers' real needs and solidify your standing as a preferred supplier.

You will be surprised at how your evaluations and priorities change. Expectations involve more than product, time, place, and price. They are the total expectations of your firm as a business partner.

The sales job changes to relationship-style selling—building trust and mutual respect, solving customer problems, helping customers succeed in what's important to them. Sales becomes less "selling to" and more "learning from" and offering solutions through transactions that are good for both parties.

Another added benefit is that you'll discover which salespeople are good at relationship-style selling. You can train the rest. Shared Expectations means changing the way you think. The process demands a difference in how your company acts. Change will be gradual.

Quality at Motorola

Some time ago, the chairman of Motorola sent a letter to all key suppliers. The message was simple: If you want to continue to be a supplier to Motorola, you must commit to pursuing the Malcolm Baldrige Award.

Don't jump to the conclusion that Motorola was taking a patriotic stand. Or that the Department of Commerce asked them to go on the stump for the quality movement. Both may be true. But the real reason was that Motorola set new, higher quality goals. They knew reaching these goals required their partners to provide defect-free products and services. Quality is an important part of their differentiation strategy and business plan. It impacts their bottom line.

Measurement at AT&T

At AT&T, we learned another lesson from Motorola. Our internal measurements showed few defects. The customer measurements painted a much different picture.

The lesson learned? Customers are not interested in nor impressed by how we measure reliability, timeliness, and quality. *Their* measurements and how *their* customers measure them *is* important. Understanding this difference is essential

Benchmarking with Customers

Another customer wanted assurance that buying service from AT&T provided a competitive advantage. Could they include this fact in their quality statement to customers? A quality-trained sales team used benchmarking tools to prove the point. The customer was able to proudly claim "Best in Class." Together, AT&T and the customer put in place a measurement to keep it that way. And in the process we earned a premium price from the customer for value-added.

Reduced Costs for an Airline

Quality knowledge helped to reduce costs for both the supplier and the customer. A large international airline found communications connections to their travel agent partners were not being installed on a timely basis. The airline's perception was that it was a telephone company problem! Together, the airline and AT&T used quality techniques to map the process, determine the requirements, and identify, count, and fix the defects. Then we continued the measurement to be sure it stayed that way. We changed the airline's perceptions. It was a joint problem. The process was not "ours" or "theirs." It was a single process owned and operated by both! When it didn't work, both lost money. Using the quality process satisfied the customer and retained the business. The net of it? More profit, better service, less cost for the customer.

Examples are numerous. But put simply, quality knowledge and ability pays off in:

- •Customer satisfaction
- •Market share
- •Profitability

2

THE SHARED
EXPECTATIONS PROCESS

THE DISCOVERY OF SHARED EXPECTATIONS

In coaching our people in the Shared Expectations process, we often emphasize the need to manage expectations at all levels of the buying continuum. We know the only way to do this is to understand fully what is expected. What we need is a good process. Judging a professional diver in the Olympics would be impossible without expectations. The judges and the contestants must both know what is expected. They also need measurements to keep score. The same is true of expectations of business partners!

Success in business requires knowing the expectations of customers. Meeting them is not enough. Exceeding them is essential. This requires a process to identify expectations. It requires a way to measure performance. Suppliers, as partners, also have expectations and those expectations need to be communicated, measured, and understood.

IMPLEMENTING THE SHARED
EXPECTATIONS PROCESS

We were fortunate that a customer suggested we formally sit down and discuss expectations—theirs and ours! It was a great opportunity to use the quality process to develop a new tool that evolved into the Shared Expectations process. We have used this approach with hundreds of customers. We have also used it extensively internally. The following steps are guidelines for implementing this process. You can make them as simple or complex as you wish, depending on how you operate and the requirements of your customers. What you see here has been greatly simplified to include only the main thoughts. The more staff and control requirements you or your customer have, the more complex your process will be.

STEP 1: SET UP THE MEETING

Suggest a joint, one-day (6 to 8 hours) meeting to your customer. The objective is to explore what the customer expects from the business relationship and what you expect from the customer relationship. Use the following outline to gain the customer's acceptance and commitment to participate. Tell your customer:

- You want to go beyond the typical customer/ supplier relationship that exists today to build the foundation for a long-term partnership.

- You and your associates have found and tailored a proven process to facilitate this objective.

- This process will help you and them identify each others' expectations. You will both benefit by knowing, understanding, and aligning each others' expectations.

- You will both be able to prioritize expectations and independently and jointly evaluate performance against these expectations.

- You will both identify ways to improve performance and build action programs that work.

STEP 2: EXPLAIN THE SHARED EXPECTATIONS PROCESS

Commit to a continuous process that includes follow-up, communication, regular meetings, and a way of keeping score. This is not a one-time shot. Tell your customer:

- Shared Expectations is an information-gathering dialogue. It is a negotiating process—a planning effort.

- The process includes measurement or grading. The idea is to identify gaps or mismatches in how you perceive each other's performance.

- The meeting will result in a workable action plan that includes action items with established target dates.

- You and your associates will arrange regular meetings to report on progress in closing gaps.

Or, instead of following this outline, just send a copy of this book with this note: "What do you think about this idea?"

STEP 3: PREPARE FOR THE MEETING

The Shared Expectations meeting requires careful preparation. Avoid oversimplification. Here is a checklist that can help:

- Jointly select who, from both customer and supplier, should attend.

- Choose a place. You need two conference rooms.

- Use a facilitator. If your company is not large enough to have someone internally, find one elsewhere. Be sure your facilitator is quality-smart and knows how to use quality tools and techniques such as:

  ➤ brainstorming

  ➤ multivoting

  ➤ conducting quality improvement meetings

- Provide the customer with written material. Include information about the process, goals and objectives, and suggested areas of dialogue such as:

  ➤ What are your expectations in these areas? (List of areas)

  ➤ What expectations are most important to you? (Prioritization)

  ➤ How would you rate our present performance in meeting your expectations? (Scoring)

  ➤ Tell us how/where we can improve. What would be considered as improvement? (Action plan)

  ➤ Where can we work together to improve our performance? (Action plan)

STEP 4: CONDUCT THE MEETING

Start the meeting as a joint session. Follow this outline:

1. Describe the Shared Expectations process using material you developed earlier in steps 1 and 2. Gain a mutual understanding of the process. A handout would be great!

2. Relate and/or develop the benefits of the Shared Expectations process in the meeting. The list will look something like this:

   ➤ Provides a tried and proven process for beginning or enhancing partnership

   ➤ Puts wheels to our commitment to customer satisfaction

   ➤ Helps to assure "first things first"

   ➤ Stimulates creative "out-of-the-box" thinking

   ➤ Improves the quality of both parties' products and services

3. Discuss each others' values, visions, and mission statements. You might suggest that each of you bring these in writing for discussion.

4. Jointly develop a list of expectations of the meeting. (You will test this list of expectations at the end of the meeting.)

5. Try warm-up exercises to get things moving. You may also need to have a *short* venting session to get pent-up feelings out in the open. Use this only if necessary and keep it to 5 or 10 minutes. The facilitator then ceremoniously "throws away" these problems, indicating that this meeting is an opportunity to begin to remove these feelings and their root causes.

6. Develop some ground rules. You see these posted in most conference rooms that quality teams use. The group list will look something like this:

   ➤ All team members are equal.

   ➤ Respect everyone. Limit criticism to ideas only.

   ➤ Be candid.

   ➤ Be open-minded.

➤ Keep confidential things confidential.

➤ Do not allow interruptions.

➤ Give all team members equal chance to participate.

➤ Organize the team (reporter, moderator, etc.)

7. Assign these two questions to each team for discussion:

➤ *What do we expect of our business partner/supplier?*

The focus of this question is on your business partner.

➤ *What do we think our business partner/supplier expects of us?*

The focus of this question is on yourself.

8. Explain that each team does the following after identifying expectations. (These are repeated in steps 7 and 8 later in this chapter.)

➤ Use a voting technique to prioritize the expectations.

➤ Clarify and consolidate statements before prioritization.

➤ Using a scale of 1 to 5 or 1 to 10, score the perception of current performance.

➤ Next, determine an expected or desired target score for each expectation.

STEP 5: SEPARATE THE TEAMS

Assign the customer team to one room and your team to the other. You will need all of the usual things in these rooms—except telephones! Off-site locations work best.

STEP 6: IDENTIFY EXPECTATIONS

Brainstorm to identify expectations on the two issues assigned in part 7 of step 4 and repeated here.

- *What do we expect of our business partner/supplier?*

  The focus of this question is on your business partner.

- *What do we think our business partner/supplier expects of us?*

  The focus of this question is on yourself.

STEP 7: CLARIFY, CONSOLIDATE, AND PRIORITIZE

Clarify, consolidate, and prioritize the information your team developed in step 6. Use multivoting or another technique

STEP 8: SCORE PERCEIVED AND TARGETED PERFORMANCES

Use a scale of 1 to 5 (or if it makes you feel better, 1 to 10) to determine:

- the desired level of performance
- the perceived level of performance

STEP 9: RECONVENE THE TEAMS

- Meet in a combined session and explain and discuss expectations. Include the scores and the justification. The lists can be quite different and very telling in their candor. In the discussion, take care to calibrate the scores. Ask such questions as:

  ➤ What does a score of 2 mean to you?

➤ How does a score of 4 differ from 3?

➤ What do we need to do to achieve the top score of 5?

- Evaluate and analyze all four lists. Correlation may reveal some significant differences. For example, one team may have listed a certain expectation as a high priority while the other team did not.

- The combined team now determines if any new information was developed in this discussion that will result in changed perceptions. Reprioritization may be appropriate.

STEP 10: DEVELOP WHAT TO MEASURE AND HOW TO MEASURE IT

The whole team must work here to fulfill the promise of enhancing the relationship. *Do not shortchange this part of the meeting.* After an active discussion, this may seem dull and boring, but stick with it! Here are the necessary activities:

1. Establish a representative and *workable measurement system.* Remember that these measures relate to the already identified expectations. You are not deciding *what* to measure, but the *unit* of measure. Here are some examples of units of measurement, accuracy, timeliness, conformance, and so on.

   ➤ 100 percent queuing accuracy of parts delivered in just-in-time systems. (Accuracy)

   ➤ 99.8 percent of all invoices received within 10 days of delivery. (Conformance)

   ➤ 100 percent of all telephone calls received before 3 p.m. returned the same day. (Timeliness)

➤ 99.3 percent of product information inquiries met within 3 business days. (Timeliness)

2. Now that the unit of measurement is established, you must determine:

➤ The frequency of measurement: hourly, daily, weekly, monthly, and so on.

➤ How to make the measurement and who measures. This involves looking at methods and procedures to determine what must be done to get the metrics.

3. Test to determine that accurate measurement is possible and meets these criteria:

➤ It helps to manage the process effectively.

➤ It promotes improved customer satisfaction.

➤ The value of measurement exceeds the difficulty of getting the measurement information.

STEP 11: DEVELOP THE DETAILED ACTION PLAN

In this step you are *not* determining expectations. You have already done this. You are now determining the actions that will lead to success and identifying the milestones along the way. Here are the elements:

• Determine a time frame for the next "look" (3 months, 6 months, etc.).

• Establish an expected score for each expectation at these intervals or milestones.

• Establish the target score. This is the expected performance resulting from the improvement activities. For example, at 6 months, the target score is 99.8 percent on-time delivery. Milestone targets are: At 2 months, 99.1 percent and at 4 months, 99.5 percent. The idea is continuous improvement toward meeting the expectation.

You still have work to do! You must determine the *what*, *who*, and *when*.

- Identify exactly *what* actions are required. For example, reconfigure voice mail and electronic mail to page the account representative automatically. Purchase an additional delivery truck and hire a driver to increase delivery frequency. In this step, you may also need to identify small or minor activities necessary to complete the major item.

- Determine *who* owns the process and is responsible for each and every action.

- Finally, *when* will the action be completed?

You are nearing the finish line. *Don't close the meeting unless you have a workable action plan!*

STEP 12: WRAP UP THE MEETING

Now is the time to revisit the participants' expectations of the meeting (identified in step 4).

- Did you meet those expectations?

- Is any follow-up action required?

  ➤ As an option, you may want participants to complete a questionnaire to evaluate the usefulness of the meeting. Ask them for ways to make future meetings more effective.

- Schedule the next meeting before you conclude.

3

THE FOLLOW-UP PLAN

Now that the meeting is over, don't be tempted to quit yet. While the information is fresh, determine the resources you need within your organization to reach the target measurement in each of the expectations. Even if your company is small, you must develop and document this important part of the internal support plan. *You waste your time if you do not develop the internal action and support plan.*

This is a good time to talk about extending the team. Think of it as a form of team selling. You need to bring the necessary resources of your company to bear on meeting expectations. The sales force can fix sales problems. Marketing, production, shipping, billing, service, and even top management will have to fix others.

You will not meet customers' expectations unless the entire extended team is committed. They must understand not only *what* the expectations are, but *why* they are the expectations. These are best expressed as:

- benefits the customer receives when the supplier meets the expectations

- rewards for the company and the extended team in satisfying these expectations.

Teamwork is essential for meeting expectations. The extended team will better cooperate if the members understand the process used to identify the customer expectations.

You will succeed only if your plan is in writing. The plan must clearly identify the owner of the process to improve, the steps to take, and the dates that each step starts and ends. This includes deciding how to measure success and the activity. It is the *who, what, how,* and *when* of success.

Approach your meeting expectations plan as though you were pulling together the resources for making a large complex sales proposal:

- Identify *who* is critical to the success of the extended team. In some instances, the extended team requires the involvement, support, and participation of top management. Later, including members of the extended team in the process will be appropriate and productive.

- Be sure that the appropriate people are taking measurements, and monitoring and tracking. A good plan includes gathering and charting the data in a systematic way.

- Design and execute a good communication plan to keep all of the stakeholders informed. You must determine *how* the team will communicate. Include formal meetings, but compare notes frequently. Don't wait for a formal meeting to touch base.

Finally, one sure way of making this process work is to tie the extended team compensation to meeting customer expectations based on customer satisfaction measurements.

Build on your successes. What satisfies one customer is likely to satisfy many.

Taking the first step is always the hardest. In the next chapter, we will cover some ways to get started that are easy and natural.

4

USING SHARED
EXPECTATIONS WITH VENDORS

A GOOD WAY TO START

Invite one of your key vendors to participate with you as the customer. Follow the same process outlined in Chapter 2.

Use the experience of this first meeting to develop your program and to sharpen your skills. The benefits of working with a business partner are numerous. You will help them to be a better supplier. That in turn will help you to improve your service and quality to your customers, especially the first customer to participate with you.

Using the Shared Expectations process internally is another good way to practice and get ready for working with your customers. In the sales force, this might be a shared expectations meeting of the account team and their support services group. This will provide you with experience. You should follow all steps of the process.

AGENDA FOR A ONE-DAY MEETING

Here is a suggested agenda for your meeting based on the information in steps 4 through 12 in Chapter 2.

What	**Who**
1. Open	Facilitator
2. List the meeting objectives	Facilitator and group
3. Jointly determine ground rules	Facilitator and group
4. Review brainstorming guidelines	Facilitator and group
5. Separate the group into a customer team and a supplier team	Facilitator and group
6. Develop expectations	Customer team and supplier team in separate rooms

- Questions for the customer:

    ➤ What do we expect of the supplier?

    ➤ What do we think the supplier expects of us?

- Questions for the supplier:

    ➤ What do we expect of the customer?

    ➤ What do we think the customer expects of us?

7. Organize and score the list of expectations	Customer team and supplier team in separate rooms

- Consolidate and clarify the expectations.

- Prioritize the expectations.

- Assign a score indicating the current performance on each expectation.

- Assign a Target Score expected on each expectation.

8. Discuss expectations   Facilitator and group
   and scoring

- The spokesperson for each group presents scoring and rationale.

- Compare and correlate the lists for the two pairs of questions

- Identify the gaps

- Reprioritize the expectations

9. Develop the measure-   Facilitator and group
   ment plan

10. Develop a detailed   Facilitator and group
    action plan

11. Agree on agenda and   Facilitator and group
    date for the next
    meeting

CHOOSING A FACILITATOR

The facilitator is essential to the success of your meetings. You cannot perform this function yourself. The facilitator must be viewed as neutral and impartial to the customer and to yourself.

When selecting a facilitator, look for one who is quality-trained. That means he or she understands the recognized processes and tools and will be able to teach you as well. Be sure to check on style and the ability to warm up the participants.

Here is a checklist for engaging a facilitator:

- Experienced in facilitation
  - ➤ good at getting full participation

> ➤ keeps the meeting on track

> ➤ sensitive to feelings and accurately reflects them to the group

> ➤ listens carefully and accurately restates questions when necessary

> ➤ alert to the need to suggest alternate approaches, methods, and procedures

> ➤ knows how to reach consensus

- Knowledgeable about the quality process

  > ➤ familiar with tools

  > ➤ familiar with terms

  > ➤ capable of training

  > ➤ able to use the tools in a team environment

- Demonstrates conflict resolution skills

A PLACE TO MEET

Planning for the physical space for the meeting is important. Take care of all of the things below to assure a productive meeting environment:

THE MEETING ROOM

Away is the key word:

- away from either of your offices

- away from telephones—including cellular phones

- away from fax machines

- away from all interruptions

You need two rooms. One must be large enough for the entire group. The second is a break-out room and can be smaller. The tables in both rooms should be U-shaped.

EQUIPMENT AND MATERIALS

The best tools are the overhead projector and easel board. Put two easels in the main room and one in the break-out room. Make sure each room has plenty of paper and multicolored markers.

You will need pins or masking tape for hanging easel sheets. If everyone does not know everyone else, have cards for making name tents.

TOOLS

Three important tools you can use to help make your meetings more productive are:

- brainstorming
- multivoting
- benchmarking

And there are many more! Here is some brief information about these tools.

Brainstorming

This is top-of-the-head, "strawman," out-of-the-box, out-loud thinking—on paper and out in the open. It is a great way to get a meeting going. Here are some rules for conducting a brainstorming session:

1. State the question(s) and write it on the easel or blackboard so everyone can see it.

2. Allow a few minutes for people to think about the question(s).

3. Encourage a large number of thoughts and ideas.

4. Encourage free thinking. Remember this is top-of-the-head thinking.

5. One person is the scribe. Don't judge the ideas. Just state them and write them down. There is no such thing here as a "bad" idea or thought.

6. Do not allow discussion of ideas during brainstorming.

7. Encourage everyone to participate and be sure that all get an equal chance.

8. List all the ideas and keep them where all can see.

9. Build on others' thoughts and ideas.

Multivoting

Think of this as prioritizing. What are the most important expectations? Here are the key steps in this process.

1. Use the easel sheets or blackboard to review the list of expectations. Explain that the idea is to prioritize.

2. Take the first vote. Each person can vote on any or all items. But only one vote per item.

3. Mark the items (star, circle, or highlight) that receive the larger numbers of votes. Establish a cutoff point that represents the majority of participants.

4. Now take the second vote. Narrow the field by allowing each person to vote a number of times equal to one-half the number of items being considered. For example, if the list has ten items, each person gets five votes. The rule of one vote per item applies.

5. Repeat steps 3 and 4 until your list is down to four or five items—never more than ten.

Benchmarking

Benchmarking is a very complex process. It is useful only if you take the time to learn the process and apply it properly. It is the subject of many excellent books and beyond the scope of this one, but a brief introduction is appropriate.

Benchmarking identifies a specific process or operation and compares it to one elsewhere. This "elsewhere" can be internal, other companies, and often even outside your industry. Benchmarking uses specific processes to compare and determine the "best-in-class." To do this right requires research, measurement, and planning.

The Malcolm Baldrige National Quality Award criteria offers the best explanation of why you should benchmark:

> *Benchmarks offer the opportunity to achieve significant improvements based on adoption or adaptation of current best practice ... benchmarks represent a clear challenge to "beat the best," thus encouraging major improvements rather than only incremental refinements of existing approaches.*[2]

The time you spend learning about this process is well worth the effort. You will gain a new perspective when you measure yourself against the best. You will find new ideas and develop new ways of doing things that will help you be the "best." See Further Reading at the end of this book for suggested readings on benchmarking.

5

THE BUYING CONTINUUM

Think of a buying continuum as a 45° line on a typical graph with x and y axes as shown in Figure 1. Usually, business decisions move along this continuum until the final decision is made. Not so long ago, people thought that the decision maker in many cases was the person at the top of this continuum, usually the CEO. Some even thought that the way to close a sale quickly was to start at the top. We have seen this lead to disaster too often to even consider it.

In large companies many people influence the buying decision. Often, the first person on the buying continuum is the analyst. Analysts are hired to do just what their title suggests: analyze! We always assigned a team member to work with the analysts to ensure awareness of our products and services. Analysts may be in the purchasing organization, but more frequently they work in operations.

Analysts usually report their findings to the next person on the buying continuum, complete with recommendations. The analysts not only analyze, but frequently also influence and recommend actions.

People between the analyst and the decision maker on the buying continuum usually act on these recommendations by engaging in dialogue with the suppliers. These people usually are involved in using or applying the product. The discussion centers on verification, deliverables, price, and terms. And it is here that the real decision is made. It may not be viewed initially as the "final decision," but in most cases, it is exactly that. This person on the buying continuum is referred to as the "recommender."

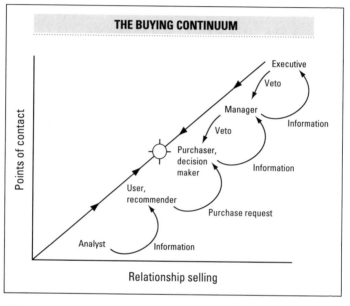

Figure 1

The next step on the buying continuum is usually decision making. That step may be a long way from the top of the organization, especially in large companies. The decision maker is usually determined by the company's schedule of authorizations, which defines the amount each person is authorized to spend on a single purchase or contract. Those who believe that anyone above this person is the real decision maker seriously misjudge the situation. Those above the decision maker actually have the power of veto. They veto the decisions of the decision makers about as often as the government vetoes bills or other projects—not very often!

What does the buying continuum have to do with shared expectations? Understanding this continuum leads quickly to the realization that the Shared Expectations process can take place at every one of these junctures, including the veto.

The power of veto, especially for important decisions, is usually the prerogative of senior management. This mandates that the Shared Expectations process must involve top management. You will be amazed at how using the Shared Expectations process results in "win-win" even at this level. This is not just another top-level call. But, it will be for those who do not use this or some similar process. You obviously need to carefully select the accounts with which you will involve senior management. Your largest and most important accounts are clearly candidates.

Using this process at all levels of the buying continuum helps you to focus your recommendations on customer objectives and needs. Your customer has helped you write the sales proposal. You know what the expectations are and you demonstrate how they are being met. Benefits have already been defined and are ready to be included in your proposal.

You will be successful in this process only if you truly believe that everyone is important to the sale.

6

SUMMARY

LESSONS LEARNED

- You will be surprised at the differences in evaluations and priorities. Expectations involve more than product, time, place, and price. They are the total expectation of your firm as a business partner.

- Not all sales people are a good fit for relationship-style selling. You will discover who is and who isn't a good fit.

- Shared Expectations means changing the way you think. Your company must act differently. But, change will be gradual.

- You will find new and creative ways to use Shared Expectations. It works in business, in your civic activities, in your personal life, and in any negotiating situation.

- You will get more than you ever thought possible as you transform vendors and suppliers into partners.

- You will have a process for assuring continuity on your key accounts when the players change.

- The Shared Expectations process will become the primary tool to use for meaningful joint account planning.

- You will use the Shared Expectations process to establish common goals and objectives. It will be your road map to building strategic partnerships.

- This tool will help you get to the root cause of problems. It will retain customers, strengthen relationships, and help you to grow accounts.

ADDED BENEFITS

- You can use the Shared Expectations process to set the target benchmark the customer will use to measure suppliers. And you will be the first to know and can be the first to meet the target requirement.

- This tool is an excellent way to revive an inactive account. By using the Shared Expectations process creatively, you will find a way.

- You will be surprised at how this process can help you to determine strategies for penetrating competitors' accounts. Can you imagine what you could learn that your competition might not know, especially if you discover this tool first!

ONE FINAL NOTE

Working hard at quality improvement doesn't always result in the kind of change customers need, appreciate, or even notice. You have to know their expectations. You must monitor them constantly. You must know their perceptions. You must aim your quality efforts squarely at what they want and value. Your customers don't really care how much you know until they know how much you care.

NOTES

1. ODI, 25 Mall Road, Burlington, Mass. 01803.
2. Malcolm Baldrige National Quality Award criteria.

FURTHER READING

Robert C. Camp, *Benchmarking: The Search for Industry Best Practices* (Milwaukee: Quality Press, 1989).

Will Kaydos, *Measuring, Managing, and Maximizing Performance* (Portland, Ore.: Productivity Press, 1991).

Michael Michalko, *Thinkertoys: A Handbook of Business Creativity for the 90's* (Berkeley, Calif.: Ten Speed Press, 1991).

Peter R. Scholtes, *The TEAM Handbook* (Madison, Wis.: Joiner Associates, Inc., 1988).

Tennessee Associates USA, Inc., *Quality Management for Marketing and Sales*, 1990.

ABOUT THE AUTHOR

Wayne A. Little is vice president of technology for the Kansas City Area Development Council. Prior to joining this not-for-profit organization, he was a sales vice president for national accounts at AT&T. He managed a large sales organization, working and consulting with the largest companies in the Midwest.

During his career, his assignments included managing service groups, publishing operations, product management, market management, sales operations, and sales management.

Little received his B.A. from the University of Tulsa and his M.B.A. from Oklahoma City University.

Wayne A. Little, 140 East Loch Lloyd Parkway, Bolton, Missouri 64012.

PRAISE FOR THE MANAGEMENT MASTER SERIES

"A rare information resource.... Each book is a gem; each set of six books a basic library.... Handy guides for success in the '90s and the new millennium."

Otis Wolkins
Vice President Quality Services/Marketing
Administration, GTE

"Productivity Press has provided a real service in its *Management Master Series*. These little books fill the huge gap between the 'bites' of oversimplified information found in most business magazines and the full-length books that no one has enough time to read. They have chosen very important topics in quality and found well-known authors who are willing to hold themselves within the 'one plane trip's worth' length limitation. Every serious manager should have a few of these in their reading backlog to help keep up with today's new management challenges."

C. Jackson Grayson, Jr.
Chairman, American Productivity & Quality Center

"The *Management Master Series* takes the Cliffs Notes approach to management ideas, with each monograph a tight 50 pages of remarkably meaty concepts that are defined, dissected, and contextualized for easy digestion."

Industry Week

"A concise overview of the critical success factors for today's leaders."

Quality Digest

"A wonderful collection of practical advice for managers."

Edgar R. Fiedler
Vice President and Economic Counsellor,
The Conference Board

"A great resource tool for business, government, and education."

Dr. Dennis J. Murray
President, Marist College

PRODUCTIVITY PRESS, Dept. BK, PO Box 13390, Portland, OR 97213-0390
Telephone: 1-800-394-6868   Fax: 1-800-394-6286

THE MANAGEMENT MASTER SERIES

The Management Master Series offers business managers leading-edge information on the best contemporary management practices. Written by respected authorities, each short "briefcase book" addresses a specific topic in a concise, to-the-point presentation, using both text and illustrations. These are ideal books for busy managers who want to get the whole message quickly.

Set 1. Great Management Ideas

Management Alert: Don't Reform—Transform!
Michael J. Kami
Transform your corporation: adapt faster, be more productive, perform better.

Vision, Mission, Total Quality: Leadership Tools for Turbulent Times
William F. Christopher
Build your vision and mission to achieve world class goals.

The Power of Strategic Partnering
Eberhard E. Scheuing
Take advantage of the strengths in your customer-supplier chain.

New Performance Measures
Brian H. Maskell
Measure service, quality, and flexibility with methods that address your customers' needs.

Motivating Superior Performance
Saul W. Gellerman
Use these key factors—non-monetary as well as monetary—to improve employee performance.

Doing and Rewarding: Inside a High-Performance Organization
Carl G. Thor
Design systems to reward superior performance and encourage productivity.

PRODUCTIVITY PRESS, Dept. BK, PO Box 13390, Portland, OR 97213-0390
Telephone: 1-800-394-6868   Fax: 1-800-394-6286

Set 2. Total Quality

The 16-Point Strategy for Productivity and Total Quality
William F. Christopher/Carl G. Thor
Essential points you need to know to improve the performance of your organization.

The TQM Paradigm: Key Ideas That Make It Work
Derm Barrett
Get a firm grasp of the world-changing ideas beyond the Total Quality movement.

Process Management: A Systems Approach to Total Quality
Eugene H. Melan
Learn how a business process orientation will clarify and streamline your organization's capabilities.

Practical Benchmarking for Mutual Improvement
Carl G. Thor
Discover a down-to-earth approach to benchmarking and building useful partnerships for quality.

Mistake-Proofing: Designing Errors Out
Richard B. Chase and Douglas M. Stewart
Learn how to eliminate errors and defects at the source with inexpensive *poka-yoke* devices and staff creativity.

Communicating, Training, and Developing for Quality Performance
Saul W. Gellerman
Gain quick expertise in communication and employee development basics.

PRODUCTIVITY PRESS, Dept. BK, PO Box 13390, Portland, OR 97213-0390
Telephone: 1-800-394-6868   Fax: 1-800-394-6286

Set 3. Customer Focus

Designing Products and Services That Customers Want
Robert King

Here are guidelines for designing customer-exciting products and services to meet the demands for continuous improvement and constant innovation to satisfy customers.

Creating Customers for Life
Eberhard E. Scheuing

Learn how to use quality function deployment to meet the demands for continuous improvement and constant innovation to satisfy customers.

Building Bridges to Customers
Gerald A. Michaelson

From the priceless value of a single customer to balancing priorities, Michaelson delivers a powerful guide for instituting a customer-based culture within any organization.

Delivering Customer Value: It's Everyone's Job
Karl Albrecht

This volume is dedicated to empowering people to deliver customer value and aligning a company's service systems.

Shared Expectations: Sustaining Customer Relationships
Wayne A. Little

How to create a process for sharing expectations and building lasting and profitable relationships with customers and suppliers that incorporates performance goals and measures.

Service Recovery: Fixing Broken Customers
Ron Zemke

Here are the guidelines for developing a customer-retaining service recovery system that can be a strategic asset in a company's total quality effort.

PRODUCTIVITY PRESS, Dept. BK, PO Box 13390, Portland, OR 97213-0390
Telephone: 1-800-394-6868   Fax: 1-800-394-6286

Set 4. Leadership (available November, 1995)

Leading the Way to Organization Renewal
Burt Nanus
How to build and steer a continually renewing and transforming organization by applying a vision to action strategy.

Checklist for Leaders
Gabriel Hevesi
Learn to focus day-to-day decisions and actions, leadership, communications, team building, planning, and efficiency.

Creating Leaders for Tomorrow
Karl Albrecht
How to mobilize all the intelligence of the organization to create value for customers.

Total Quality: A Framework for Leadership
D. Otis Wolkins
Consider the problems and opportunities in today's world of changing technology, global competition, and rising customer expectations in terms of the leadership role.

From Management to Leadership
Lawrence M. Miller
A visionary analysis of the qualities required of leaders in today's business: vision and values, enthusiasm for customers, teamwork, and problem-solving skills at all levels.

High Performance Leadership: Creating Value in a World of Change
Leonard R. Sayles
Examine the need for leadership involvement in work systems and operations technology to meet the increasing demands for short development cycles and technologically complex products and services.

PRODUCTIVITY PRESS, Dept. BK, PO Box 13390, Portland, OR 97213-0390
Telephone: 1-800-394-6868   Fax: 1-800-394-6286

ABOUT PRODUCTIVITY PRESS

Productivity Press exists to support the continuous improvement of American business and industry.

Since 1983, Productivity has published more than 100 books on the world's best manufacturing methods and management strategies. Many Productivity Press titles are direct source materials translated for the first time into English from industrial leaders around the world.

The impact of the Productivity publishing program on Western industry has been profound. Leading companies in virtually every industry sector use Productivity Press books for education and training. These books ride the cutting edge of today's business trends and include books on total quality management (TQM), corporate management, Just-In-Time manufacturing process improvements, total employee involvement (TEI), profit management, product design and development, total productive maintenance (TPM), and system dynamics.

To get a copy of the full-color catalog, call 800-394-6868 or fax 800-394-6286.

To view sample chapters and see the complete line of books, visit the Productivity Press online catalog on the Internet at *http://www.ppress.com/*

Productivity Press titles are distributed to the trade by National Book Network, 800-462-6420

TO ORDER: Write, phone, or fax Productivity Press, Dept. BK, P.O. Box 13390, Portland, OR 97213-0390, phone 800-394-6868, fax 800-394-6286. Send check or charge to your credit card (American Express, Visa, MasterCard accepted).

U.S. ORDERS: Add $5 shipping for first book, $2 each additional for UPS surface delivery. We offer attractive quantity discounts for bulk purchases of individual titles; call for more information.

ORDER BY E-MAIL: Order 24 hours a day from anywhere in the world. Use either address:
To order: *service@ppress.com*
To view online catalog on the Internet and/or to order:
  http://www.ppress.com/

INTERNATIONAL ORDERS: Write, phone, or fax for quote and indicate shipping method desired. For international callers, telephone number is 503-235-0600 and fax number is 503-235-0909. Prepayment in U.S. dollars must accompany your order (checks must be drawn on U.S. banks). When quote is returned with payment, your order will be shipped promptly by the method requested.

NOTE: Prices are in U.S. dollars and are subject to change without notice.